FROM PAUSE
TO
Purpose

9 P's that Prepare You for Destiny

ROBIN RENEE WILSON

A special "Thank You" to my husband, Brian Wilson, for being my covering throughout this journey. I could not have made it through this season without you.

I dedicate this book to every trial, every heartache, and every storm of life I have come through. This book would not exist if it were not for the refining and perfecting that each experience provided. To God be the glory for working all things together for my good!

And after you have suffered a little while, the God of all grace who has called you to His eternal glory in Christ, will Himself restore, confirm, strengthen, and establish you.

1 PETER 5:10 (ESV)

TABLE OF CONTENTS

INTRODUCTION

୬ℓ

Beloved, I'm so excited for you! The fact that you are reading this book means you made it through your fiery trials and have been proven true. It means you have, with the help of Holy Spirit, sown some costly seeds and mastered some important lessons. A spiritual transformation has occurred in your life, and God is preparing to usher you into Purpose.

Believe me when I tell you I know the road has not been easy. I know about the bumps, bruises, tests, and trials that came to perfect you. I know about the seasons of isolation and wilderness, but I also know God is saying to you, "Well done. Prepare for Purpose!"

The Lord spoke the following words to me before sending me into Purpose: "The Harvest is ripe. I am preparing to send you forth. It's your time and it's your turn. Are you ready?" These words confirmed that I was indeed entering a long-awaited season in my life. They challenged me to leave every tear, every heartbreak, and every dismissal from man behind. I passed my tests, and now God was preparing to put a shine on me that was undeniable. A shine that said, "She's My chosen servant and she's ready."

As God said to me, I now say to you: God is preparing to send you forth. It's your time and it's your turn. Are you ready? Beloved, your past is behind you, and your future awaits. You passed your tests and now He's about to use the following 9 P's to polish you for Purpose.

What is Polishing?

The analogy of washing and waxing a car is the best way I can explain this process.

We wash our cars for the sake of cleaning them, however, sometimes a simple wash just isn't enough. Sometimes it takes a bit more elbow grease to make it shine, and even then the results leave something to be desired. An additional process is required to take the shine to a whole new level, as well as add a layer of protection between the car and the environment. This is when waxing enters the picture.

A good coat of wax enhances the beauty of a car's paintwork and protects it from the effects of weathering and aging.[1] The wax is applied in small circular motions after the car has been washed and dried. This isn't a fast process, but rather one of intentionality and detail. The wax is removed once it has dried for a short period of time. The result is a shine and a new layer of protection on another level -- one that a simple wash could never accomplish.

Beloved, you are not diminished to that of a car, but as a visual God is preparing to polish you to remove the last layer of residue from your previous seasons of refining. Yes, you shine, but He wants you to radiate His glory. The encounters you've experienced with Him were good, but there's more, there's deeper, there's higher. Seek Him in ways you've never sought Him before. Increase your time in His Word and in His presence.

---

1   "How to Wax a Car." *The Drive.Com*, 23 Sept. 2023, www.thedrive.com/cleaning-detailing/27319/how-to-wax-a-car. Accessed 5 May 2024.

It's in the experiences of more, deeper, and higher that the polish for your next season is applied. He's saying, "My child, your previous anointing isn't enough. You need more. A fresh anointing awaits. One that's weightier and shines far brighter than the one in which you've been operating. This new anointing is for your new season to lay hold of that which awaits your arrival."

Beloved, "A force to be reckoned with" is what I hear for you. Nothing will stop you. You will enter your next season mentally, spiritually, physically, and emotionally equipped to accomplish His will. You've experienced the lessons, and now the lessons are working for you. He's about to place the weight of His glory upon you, which is undeniable. Get ready to shine!

I encourage you to read this book as a roadmap designed to help navigate you into Purpose. The pages that follow will confirm, affirm, correct, and instruct many of you who find yourself in various places of polishing and perfection. A Key Points section at the end of each chapter highlights important truths to meditate on, and an In Your Quiet Time section gives you an opportunity to delve deeper into the things you've read with journaling prompts and challenges.

I pray this book blesses you beyond measure. I pray it prepares you for the mighty work God is about to accomplish through you to advance His kingdom. Beloved, the fields are ready and eagerly await your arrival.

God bless you, my Brother and my Sister.

Love,
Robin

CHAPTER 1:

PRAYER

The Power Source

If any of you lacks wisdom, let him ask of God who gives to all liberally and without reproach, and it will be given to him.

JAMES 1:5

Prayer is to the believer what gasoline is to a car. It fuels us. It is the power source by which we live our lives. It puts us in direct communication with the Father, and there we receive everything we need for life.

Colossians 4:2 tells us to devote ourselves to prayer, being watchful and thankful. To devote means to give all or a large part of our time or resources to. To devote ourselves to prayer is to pray about **everything**. It precedes and follows everything you and I attempt to accomplish. Our lives are transformed, we influence our surroundings, and we develop the stamina and confidence we need to walk boldly into Purpose.

Prayer is Vital to the Nine P's Process

A consistent prayer life is vital to the nine P's process. With it, each phase becomes more than a set of circumstances we experience. They become change agents that develop us for Purpose.

Our prayers give us access to the Kingdom of Heaven, where we receive everything we need to successfully progress through each refining process. We invite Holy Spirit to walk alongside us to strengthen us, give us wisdom, and ultimately transform us more into the likeness of our Heavenly Father.

The act of listening during prayer is just as important, if not more, than speaking. It's an act of humility that says, "God, I've spoken now I want to hear Your heart about the matter." It is Proverbs 3:5-6 in operation: Trust in the Lord with all your heart and lean not on your own understanding; in all your ways acknowledge Him, and He shall direct your paths.

Listening during prayer gives the Lord the opportunity to direct our paths with the wisdom He pours into us only as we posture ourselves to hear from Him. You'll read more about this in Chapter 4.

Key Points

· Prayer must be the power source by which we live our lives
· To devote ourselves to prayer is to pray about **everything**
· Consistent prayer is vital to the nine P's process

In Your Quiet Time

Think about your prayer life. How much time do you devote to regular communication with the Lord that consists of praying and listening? Are there areas of your prayer life you can improve upon, such as consistency or the amount of time you spend listening for Holy Spirit's response to your prayers?

CHAPTER 2:

PRESSURE

Get Ready to Look Like Him

*For our light affliction, which is but for a moment, is working
for us a far more exceeding and eternal weight of glory.*

2 CORINTHIANS 4:17

I was awakened one morning by my youngest daughter's cries for her
early morning bottle. The Lord spoke six words that turned my life up-
side down as I stood at the kitchen sink: "Get ready, get ready, get ready."
I asked, "Get ready like T.D. Jakes, Father?" "No," He replied. "Get ready
for My return." He explained that "Get ready" meant get ready to look
like Him. He explained that my ministry is one very similar to His. Beloved, I was over the moon. Who wouldn't want to hear the Almighty
God tell you He is fashioning you to look like Him and have a ministry

like His? It was an honor. I just knew my life was about to overflow with good things. Little did I know there would be a high cost.

Pressure Defined

Pressure is the God-ordained season of continuous tests and trials for the intent of purging us of everything that taints us. Pressure never destroys us, but it does squeeze us. It squeezes stuff out of us that isn't beneficial for our purpose. In the end, pressure becomes our friend, although that's the farthest adjective from our minds when it is actively working in our lives.

Our Pressure Processes are Tailormade

We each have tailor-made Pressure processes (Notice I said processes. We will experience many in this lifetime) because we each have a tailor-made purpose. God knows the specific set of circumstances and precise amount of weight that will bring us forth as pure gold. What's a struggle for me may be a cake walk for you, and vice versa. However, the emotions we experience are universal, and they are real. Despite what our pressure looks like, every one of us experiences sadness, anger, frustration, or loneliness (to name a few), and it's okay. It lets us know a work is being accomplished in us.

My Pressure process during this season consisted of three steps: Consecration, Forsaking All, and Freedom from the Opinions of Man.

Consecration

I heard the word Consecration before I experienced it. I had an idea of what the word meant, but I studied it to get a more in-depth revelation of what God was about to do in my life. I learned it meant set apart, to make or declare sacred, singled out for a special assignment, and distinguished as Holy unto the Lord. Of all the definitions, "to make or declare sacred" stood out the most. I felt special. If the Lord had favorites, I was definitely one of them. My head lifted a little higher, and I had a spring in my step. "God declares I'm sacred, I'm set apart. I'm holy unto the Lord," were my thoughts as I went about life. Then the process began.

Yes, I was set apart for a special work unto the Lord. Spiritually, I was set apart, and physically, the Lord began to set me apart. He isolated me and began to strip me of everything I depended on. It was a very lonely place. One that consisted of just me and God. No one understood what I was going through. I was around people, yet alone. I knew evolving from this place meant I had to understand how to adjust my life. I began to understand that the more I endured the process of isolation and stripping, the heavier the weight of God's glory could rest upon my life.

Beloved, He showed me the deep-rooted ugly parts of myself once I was alone and undistracted. The self-hatred I experienced from childhood drama and feelings of unworthiness were some of the things that surfaced. I felt like I was in a cocoon of darkness with just me and my experiences. It was the perfect setup for the Lord to deep-clean my soul. One by one, He undid the effects of my past and showed me a glimpse of the woman He called me to be. He assigned spiritual parents to my life who confirmed what He was up to. What God told me in private, my spiritual parents and prophets spoke out loud.

The Lord ended my Consecration season with a great display of His power. He led me to attend a conference at West Angeles Church of God in Christ. He told me to go to the altar at the end of the service. There were so many people there that the woman of God who was ministering couldn't physically lay hands on me. Instead, she extended them towards me, and immediately we both fell to the floor under the power of Holy Spirit. A spiritual transfer took place that night. One that sealed my Consecration experience and everything Holy Spirit spoke to me during this time.

Forsake All

Forsake all meant forsaking everything. Forsake everything and anything that had the potential to come between me and what God wanted to do in this season. The choice was mine. I could've settled for the measure of God I already had, but His purpose inside of me cried out for more.

Forsaking all began with my business. There was a time when I had more clients than I could handle. My appointment book always overflowed. Money was no object. I could afford to do what I wanted when I wanted.

Though my hands styled hair, ministry was never far off. Wednesday noontime Bible study was a must-attend, and Sundays were consecrated as holy unto the Lord. I thought I was doing something by holding those days sacred, but the Lord needed more. He invaded my work schedule and led me to attend church services during my working hours. It didn't matter what day or time of the week. He wanted out of the "consecrated box" I had Him in.

Although I surrendered to the Lord's will, I'd be lying if I said I wasn't afraid. He was encroaching upon my livelihood. One by one, my clients left, and I knew the reason why. It was a major stripping. I watched the very people who I thought were my source walk away, and there was nothing I could do about it. I wanted Purpose over provision. If forsaking all was what it took to walk in Purpose, I was IN. Beloved, I went from paying my bills before they were due to paying them just before they were late. I went from knowing well in advance where money was coming from to accomplish whatever needed to be done, to having to fully rely upon the Lord to supply all my needs according to His riches in glory by Christ Jesus (Philippians 4:19). I no longer trusted in my ability to meet my needs. I was forced to seek God for everything, and it didn't feel good. People who knew me prior to the Pressure process wondered what happened to me. All the while I wanted to say, "Ask God. This is all His doing."

Family & Friends

Matthew 19:29 states, And everyone who has left houses or brothers or sisters or father or mother or wife or children or lands, for My Name's sake, shall receive a hundredfold and inherit eternal life. Beloved, God brought this scripture alive during my forsaking of family and friends. There came a time when my family and I no longer worshipped together. The Lord ordered my steps to various churches to receive impartations and connect to spiritual mothers and fathers who He used to mature me. I was literally all over Los Angeles going to conferences, workshops, and services that were led by key individuals of His choosing.

Though staying in my home church and worshipping as a family was my heart's desire, God knew He could trust me with what He was doing. My husband played a major role in the household and with our girls. He made it possible for me to obey God's will for my life. Beloved, obedience is not always convenient. I knew what God wanted me to do to prepare for Purpose, and I had to cooperate with His will for my life.

Friendships

My Friendships were the last things to go. I mentioned in my previous book *(He is Who I Worship)* how the Lord stripped me of relationships that were not healthy for me--broken feathers that prohibited me from flying as high as He needed and wanted me to fly. Well, this time the Lord removed individuals from my life whom I truly considered friends. Some friendships ended as the Lord pulled me away from my business into more kingdom work. Others fell away because I no longer made them feel comfortable the closer I got to Purpose. This phase separated me from the very people I thought would go with me into my future, but God said not so. I will say that with all the falling away, God, in His mercy, allowed a select few to remain. To God be the glory!

Surrendering the Opinions of Others

I lived for the opinions of others before I entered this phase. I needed their validation, and before God delivered me, I needed them to validate His call on my life. Beloved, this is a very dangerous need because relying on others for validation makes them your master. What if they never affirm you? What if God doesn't allow them to see His call upon your life? They can't call out what they can't see. Validation is nice, but not necessary. John 2:24 says, But Jesus did not commit Himself to them because He knew all men. If He, being the Son of God, did not entrust Himself to man, why should we? Let's establish in our hearts that the Lord's validation is enough.

The Lord also set me free from the opinions of those closest to me--my family. God taught me that although my husband and children love me and want nothing but the best for me, I needed deliverance from their opinions as well. There were many occasions where the Lord instructed me to take leaps of faith that my husband and my children discouraged me from taking. Not because they didn't want to see me win, but because they didn't want to see me experience hurt or disappointment. They've been on this journey with me for a long time. They've seen my tears and heard my pain. Their discouragement, though well-intended, was not God's perfect plan. Each experience taught me that while my family's love for me is great, God's love for me is greater, and I needed to value His will over my family's efforts to protect me.

Beloved, total surrender is forsaking ALL, just like Abraham was willing to sacrifice Isaac. We must lay it all (including that thing closest to us) on the altar so He can use it for His glory. It's costly, but the benefits are rewarding.

God Knows Your Purpose Even if You Don't

The Pressure process seems like the loneliest place we could ever experience. Sometimes it can be so bad that we are tempted to doubt the love of the Father. "God, do you hear what these people are saying?" "Do you not care about the fact that my heart is breaking?" These questions often raced through my mind. Not for a minute would I compare my suffering to that of Jesus, but I can relate to Him when He cried, "Father, Father, why have You forsaken me?" But like Jesus, the Father had a much better plan in mind that involved His glory shining in my life.

Sometimes the Lord doesn't rescue us from situations we deem tragic. Notice I said, *we deem* tragic. What we see as the end of the world may not be so with the Lord. Beloved, we don't like to feel uncomfortable, so we are quick to say this is hard, too much, and call a light affliction a tragedy.

But God (our loving Father and Creator) fashioned us, and He knows what He put in us. He knows our capabilities and our tolerance levels, and while we call it "tragedy," He calls it a "minor affliction" and allows us to stay under Pressure just a little longer until His will is accomplished in our lives.

I had no idea when God spoke, "Get ready, get ready, get ready," that I was about to enter a Pressure process that would literally kill my flesh and begin a transformation process that would turn me into a new woman. A woman who looks more, sounds more, and acts more like her Heavenly Father. He's not finished with me, but I thank God for the work He has accomplished.

Key Points

- Obedience is not always convenient
- We each have tailor-made Pressure processes because we each have a tailor-made purpose
- Pressure is the God-applied weight of His glory upon our lives
- True surrender is to keep your focus on God and Him alone
- Sometimes God doesn't rescue us from situations we deem tragic

In Your Quiet Time

1. What areas are you struggling with in your Pressure process? Spend some time with Holy Spirit and ask Him what He wants to teach you.
2. Pray and ask for Holy Spirit's assistance to help you stay the course until His will is accomplished in your life.

CHAPTER 3:

PIVOT

Get on God's Frequency

"Pivoting is a necessary tweak for those of us who are on our way to Purpose. The change may be ever so slight, or a full about face, but whatever the Lord is impressing upon our spirits to change, heeding it becomes a major player on our road to Purpose."

-ROBIN RENEE

If there's one thing the 2020 global pandemic taught us, it's how to pivot. The influx of the coronavirus put life as we knew it completely on hold. Everything, even the things we took for granted, had to change. Survival meant doing things differently, and fast.

Merriam-Webster Dictionary defines pivot as an adjustment or modification for the purpose of improvement. One of the many things I learned on my journey to Purpose is the importance of pivoting to tune in to God's frequency. I needed to hear His voice over my own and over the voices that were speaking in my life. It was no longer about asking others for advice or leaning on my past successes to direct my future. I made many costly mistakes that way. God desired to change the trajectory of my life and lead me to Purpose. He extended an invitation to me to tune in to His frequency because only He had the plan. Proverbs 3:5-6 became my rock scripture as my Pivot process began: Trust in the Lord with all your heart and lean not on your own understanding; in all your ways acknowledge Him, and He shall direct your paths.

What is God's Frequency?

God's frequency is the spiritual channel that carries His voice. Worldly knowledge has no place here. It is reserved for divine knowledge that reveals divine plans, purposes, intentions, and direction. God's frequency is a supernatural frequency that holds everything we need. Jeremiah 33:3 says, Call to Me, and I will answer you, and show you great and mighty things which you do not know. Our "call" unto the Lord in this scripture is akin to us pivoting from our frequency to His, and it must become a way of life if we want to ensure we are in the center of His divine will.

How I Found God's Frequency

I discovered God's frequency at a time in my life when I was thoroughly exhausted. Have you ever seen people who do too much? Their actions and goals are all over the place. They never focus too long on one thing, yet they have their hands in a million things. That was me. I was doing too much. God spoke His will in my life--things He wanted me to do, plans

He had for me, and directions He wanted me to go. I got busy trying to make it all happen because I thought every one of those words meant it was for that moment. I was completely and utterly exhausted. God told me I was so busy being busy that I was missing Him, and I wasn't bringing Him glory.

Beloved, my ears were tuned in to my own frequency that consisted of a false belief system: busy equals productive; my clients are my livelihood; if I hear, that means I must move immediately. I was on the move for God in ministry and business, and in many cases, He hadn't told me to take one step. He merely wanted to *tell* me His plans, but I needed to ask for the timing in which He wanted me to move. I thought it meant *go* and *do.* I was frustrated, exhausted, barely making ends meet, and stressed out. God wanted me to fulfill His plans His way, and the only way I was going to do that was to tune in to His frequency and remain there. I needed to understand it wasn't an in-and-out thing; it was a lifestyle. Most importantly, I needed to remember that my gifts and callings are without repentance, so while I flowed in ministry, I missed God.

One day, I heard it was time for a change. I knew those words were big for me. They came after I whispered a silent prayer to the Lord out of sheer exhaustion: "God, I don't like where I am." That prayer ushered in an exciting change in my life. As confirmation, God sent a woman to my salon many days later, and she prophesied grace to me and gave me a five-dollar bill. The number five represents God's grace and favor. God was just waiting for me to release that prayer because He knew what He had in store for me.

The days that followed brought about exciting changes. I had the opportunity to return to my first love, Jesus Christ, because the nation was shut down. I became still, grew silent, and tuned in to God's frequency. I had time to stop, pause, and pray after I heard Him speak. He revealed details about what He wanted me to do. Everything was shut down, so I couldn't run out and start making things happen on my own. I was forced to listen and wait for His strategy, and it proved to be a great blessing.

God's Frequency Reveals Strategy

Everything God does is executed decently and in order (1 Corinthians 14:40). He's the master of organization and strategic acumen. Just look at His plan to save the world. He wasn't rash. He knew Jesus was His plan for salvation, but He didn't send Him into the world the minute Adam and Eve missed the mark. He had a strategy. He had key players in position to prepare the way for the Savior. God still worked out His master plan even when it appeared as though the enemy had the upper hand.

Likewise, Beloved, we must ask the Father to give us the strategy that allows His master plan to unfold in our lives. Like Him, we too must remain steadfast and consistent even when it appears things aren't working out the way we expect. We must also understand that though God reveals His will, the time to execute isn't always at that moment. We must operate like the people of Issachar who were described as people who understood the times and knew what Israel should do (1Chronicles 12:32). We must hear from God and seek Him for timing and strategy; otherwise, like me you'll be all over the place wearing yourself out, busy doing kingdom work but missing God.

Beloved, as people of Purpose we must be intentional, sharp, planners, and master strategists, just like our Heavenly Father. We must discern what's for now and what's for later, and it all hinges on tuning in to God's frequency.

So many wonderful things were birthed in Robin Renee Ministries because I pivoted to God's frequency. He gave me the strategy and resources to accomplish every one of them because I waited for Him.

When we pivot to God's frequency, everything prospers. Why? Because we take *ourselves* out of the picture and allow Him to take the wheel. That's when He really shows out. Let's be still and listen for God because He will answer. "We will hear a word behind us saying, 'This is the way, walk in it,' when we turn to the right or when we turn to the left" (Isaiah 30:21).

Key Points

- People of Purpose are intentional, sharp, planners, and master strategists
- Getting on God's frequency is a must if we are to abide in His perfect will
- When we hear a word from God, it's not always for right now
- Seek God for His timing and strategic direction
- Just because we're busy for God doesn't mean we're in His perfect will
- We must take time to be still and hear from God

In Your Quiet Time

1. Make a list of everything you have on your activity plate. Write "Me" or "Holy Spirit" next to each item on your list, indicating which of you inspired the activity.
2. For each item on your list that says "Me," ask Holy Spirit for the strength and power to put those things down and only focus on the activities led by Him.

3. Pray and ask Holy Spirit for forgiveness for not tuning in to His frequency. Ask Him to help you pivot from your own frequency to His.

CHAPTER 4:

POSTURE

Submission is Necessary

*"God is ready to assume full responsibility for the life wholly
yielded to Him."*

-ANDREW MURRAY

Our posture is our outward expression of our internal feelings towards a situation or person. It is a particular way of dealing with or
considering something; it's an approach or an attitude.

The Lord wanted to change how I interacted with Him, so He went
straight to the area that was the greatest hindrance, my posture towards
my husband. The Message version of Ephesians 5:22-24 reads: Wives, understand and support your husbands in ways that show your support for
Christ. The husband provides leadership to his wife the way Christ does to
His church, not by domineering but by cherishing. So just as the church

submits to Christ as He exercises such leadership, wives should likewise submit to their husbands. Beloved, the Lord was leading me to submit to Him in a greater capacity so He could do a greater work in and through me, but He had to get my relationship with my husband in order.

My posture change started when the Lord allowed me to overhear my coworker discussing what submission meant to him. It sparked my curiosity. He said his wife had to check in with him before she went anywhere and did anything. I cringed as I listened to him speak. Everything he said sounded very controlling and domineering. I wondered if Brian felt the same way. The more I thought about his answer, the more agitated I became.

Our marriage was a little rocky and in need of a spiritual boost at that time, but I didn't know where to begin. I felt in my spirit that the word submission was a key player in the rejuvenation of our relationship. We were married at the age of 23. We didn't know much about what makes for a strong relationship, but we did know divorce was not an option. We needed help.

My husband and I are headstrong individuals. We speak our minds—sometimes unapologetically. This way of communication works great on some occasions and blows up on others. As a child, my mom would always say, "Robin, you always have to have the last word," and it carried over into my marriage and became an ingredient in the recipe for disaster.

I couldn't wait to ask Brian about his thoughts. I wasn't in the house two seconds before I asked him for his take on submission. I waited anxiously for what I thought would be a drawn-out explanation. Much to my surprise, he simply said, "Just don't nag me. Let me be me and just don't nag." You see, I was the queen of nagging, and that was the cause of most of our arguments. I was so intent on trying to make Brian the godly man *I* thought he should be. I'd nag him when he didn't respond thinking that would push him into action. Instead, my nagging set him off and led to arguments. He'd yell at me, and I'd yell right back. He'd yell louder, and I'd get even louder. Beloved, it wasn't pretty.

One day, I came home from work with my hair freshly done. I was cute. An exchange occurred that at first was very insignificant. The longer we talked, the more we disagreed. The more we disagreed, the more intense our conversation became until it turned into an all-out argument. He yelled his point at me, and I yelled mine right back. It went on for at least an hour. It was heated-- literally and figuratively. I felt myself sweating during the argument but wouldn't calm down. By the time I caught a glimpse of myself in the mirror, my hair looked like I'd just gotten it blow-dried. I got so upset and sweated so badly that my freshly pressed hair turned into an afro! Beloved, I knew right then something had to change. I needed to take Brian's simple request to heart and stop nagging him. It wasn't an overnight process, but the more I submitted to his request in that area, the more I submitted in others. My countenance began to soften towards Brian and vice versa, and it ushered in a beautiful change in our marriage.

Submission was the key that unlocked the door to the next level of intimacy and friendship in our relationship. I'm sure it's the reason we're still together today. Proverbs 25:24 says, It is better to dwell in a corner of a housetop than in a house shared with a contentious woman. I was the contentious woman whose posture God was interested in changing.

Beloved, let me tell you the arguments in our home hit an all-time low when I learned when and how to speak to my husband. I had to learn to bend in submission towards him and allow him to be who he was and realize it was not my job to change him. He's God's son, and He's the only One who can bring about authentic change in any man or woman. I won't say it was easy, but my marriage was important enough that I was willing to allow the Lord to change my posture towards my husband and ultimately towards Him. The Lord began to show me areas in my relationship with Him where I was not wholly submitted when I learned how to submit to Brian. Areas such as how I handled my time, my eating, my spending, and my exercise. They were all areas of inconsistent obedience. Areas the Lord wanted and needed to change if I was going to walk fully equipped into Purpose.

Beloved, the Lord used my marriage to develop my submission to Brian and ultimately to Himself. There was no way I could truly have a good posture toward Him if my posture toward my husband was raggedy. I feel He was saying, "Now that you have submitted to your husband, you can properly submit to Me." I could never have fully walked into Purpose until the Lord changed my posture. And, glory to God, at the end of this season, Brian commented that He saw the change in me and that he didn't see me as the nagging wife anymore. Praise God for promotion! Now we enjoy regular spa treatments together and watching our favorite shows that we won't dare watch without one another. To God be the glory!

Key Points
- When God changes your posture, it's to bless you, not break you
- Your posture change will result in you looking and sounding more like Jesus
- Your posture change in the natural has reverberating effects in the spirit

In Your Quiet Time

You may not need to change your posture in submission to your spouse, but there is an area in your life where the Lord is requiring your posture to change so you can look and respond more like Him. I hear the Lord saying, "Your change of posture is to bless you, not break you." Lean into the process and receive the blessing that's waiting. You'll be surprised to see the reverberating effects it will have in your life. Take a moment and consider the following questions:

1. In what area(s) is the Lord changing your posture? List them.
2. Write a letter of encouragement to yourself. Tell yourself what you want *you* to know about your struggles, why you wrestle with them, and how you can participate with Holy Spirit to overcome them.

CHAPTER 5:

PUSH

Quitting is Not an Option

Do not let yourselves get tired of doing good. If we do not give up, we will get what is coming to us at the right time.

GALATIANS 6:9 NLV

Beloved, you know you're close to walking into Purpose when all you want to do is quit. May I share from experience that this is the time when you need to push the hardest. The process may be wearing on you, but be of good courage because those who wait on the Lord shall renew their strength; they shall mount up with wings like eagles, they shall run and not be weary, they shall walk and not faint (Isaiah 40:31).

Pushing Into Destiny

I was like a kid in a candy store as my girlfriend and I prepared to travel to Dallas, Texas to attend a Woman Thou Art Loosed Master Class. I'd received several denials for a loan to purchase a property for the ministry by this time. The rejection was beginning to wear on me, but I pushed it to the back of my mind for the sake of the conference. I wasn't about to miss my blessing.

The first two days of teaching were amazing. The Lord eased my concerns about the slow growth of my ministry and how it seemed like there was a revolving door of people coming and going. Hope rose in me as I listened to Bishop Jakes' testimony of The Potter's House's small beginnings. I was in the right place at the right time, but the real kicker came on day three.

I sensed the Lord wanted to change our seats as we entered the sanctuary that morning. He led us to the back of the house and had us sit in a row that had about five women seated who were dressed in camouflage. A friendly woman turned around and greeted us as we took our seats. We chatted for a bit until the conference began.

The air was charged with an unusual anointing that was unlike the previous days. Something was about to break forth, I could feel it. Bishop Jakes talked about Mary and Elizabeth and how Elizabeth's baby leaped in her belly when Mary entered the room. What happened next had my head spinning days after the event. A sudden pain hit my belly and I screamed. It felt like the worst labor pains. It came suddenly and hit with intensity. In an instant, every woman I spoke with in that section revealed their true identity and jumped into position. The friendly woman who sat in front of me turned around and became my midwife. She was no longer the sweet, smiling woman who spoke gently and softly to me. Her sweet, gentle voice turned loud and forceful as she yelled, "Push!" I screamed and writhed in pain as I lay on the floor in a full birthing position pushing out Purpose. The women in camouflage jumped into position as intercessors. They surrounded me--some praying in the Spirit while others spoke words of encouragement as they witnessed the birthing process.

I wasn't the only one giving birth to Purpose that day. There were a few of us screaming and pushing. I heard Bishop Jakes say at one point, "You hear that? Their babies are leaping. They're giving birth." Beloved, by the end of the conference, I understood why the Lord changed our seats. He had every woman strategically positioned to assist me in pushing out destiny. This experience gave me new hope, increased faith, and the resolve to see God's purpose and plan for the ministry *He* gave me come to fruition. My friend who witnessed the birth later told me the Lord spoke to her and told her to sow a seed to the baby I had just birthed. Won't He do it!

The Push Afterglow

The Push afterglow places you in a new realm of authority and favor when it comes upon you. You begin to walk in places you've never been able to walk in before, and people see and treat you differently. The Push afterglow tells people you've been in the presence of the Lord. Like Moses' face radiated the glory of God when he descended from the mountaintop with the 10 Commandments. People who come out of the Push radiate an unmistakable glow that causes our enemies to behave and people to stare in wonder.

The Lord led us to a particular restaurant before heading to the airport to return home. It was an unruly scene inside. The owner was on a major tirade. He spoke rudely and threw customers out of his restaurant, left and right. It was the last stop before we got to the airport; otherwise, we would've left before he could throw us out. He studied me for a minute as we approached the counter. I braced myself for what he would say. Much to my surprise, I heard, "Hello, Beautiful. I just love your smile. What can I do for you?" "You talking to me?" I thought. I said hello and proceeded to place my order. Beloved, He was kind the entire time! He brought our food to the table himself, and with a smile. We watched this man belittle customers and throw them out of his restaurant, but he treated us differently. The Spirit of the Lord revealed that my pushing out Purpose was so powerful that it influenced the way people responded to me. It was the glory of God on my life that ushered me into a new realm of favor with God and favor with man.

We found ourselves surrounded by a crowd of people on their way back to Los Angeles as we entered the airport terminal. Among the crowd was a well-known pastor and first lady who led a megachurch in Los Angeles. I noticed the first lady staring at me as if the Lord was speaking to her about me. I didn't think much about it until I looked away and looked back again, only to find she was still staring. My girlfriend encouraged me to approach her to introduce myself. I'm not the type of person at a loss for words, so when I felt myself scrambling for what I would say, I knew it wasn't time. Beloved, the Lord showed me this couple for many years and told me we'd do kingdom work together, but I sensed in my spirit that moment was not the right time for the connection. But what I do believe is that the Push of Purpose brought me closer to that moment. I believe, when the time is right, the Lord will make the connection for us to work in the fields of His Kingdom together, and it will be powerful.

Key Points

- You know you're closer to Purpose when all you want to do is quit
- God assigns people to help you birth your destiny
- Your destiny is so powerful that it will influence the way people respond to you
- The afterglow of birthing destiny will cause you to walk in a new realm of favor
- Don't get ahead of the Lord. Wait on Him to make divine connections

In Your Quiet Time

Beloved, you're at the point where you must push the hardest. Giving up now would forfeit all the lessons you've mastered before this point. Lean into Holy Spirit and allow His strength to become your strength. Take some time and answer the following questions:

1. Do you feel like giving up right now? Are you tired of the journey and feel like you have nothing left to give? Journal your answer.
2. Meditate on Isaiah 40:31. Listen for what Holy Spirit speaks to you regarding everything you wrote above.

CHAPTER 6

PERFECTION

The Grading of a Diamond

"Perfection is the spiritual grading process the Lord takes us through to reveal His accomplished work in us."

-ROBIN RENEE

"Robin, I'm making you into a diamond." The Lord spoke these seven words to me before I entered my season of Perfection. Truth be told, I got a little nervous. The words sounded good, but I'd been in covenant with the Lord long enough to know He was about to take me through something, and chances were it wasn't going to feel good. I was right.

Becoming A Diamond

A diamond isn't impressive in its raw state. Its beauty is revealed and its value skyrockets only after it evolves from a rigorous cleaning and refining process. This process prepares the diamond for public presentation. Beloved, I believe the Lord likened me to a diamond because He took me through a refinement process that cut away dead things in my life that weighed me down. His goal was to allow the hidden person trapped under the dirt and grime of life experiences to burst forth. It felt like a continuous cycle of cutting and polishing. I cried, asked how much longer, and felt sorry for myself. Beloved, He took me through, but it was all for Purpose. *His* purpose for my life. His grace was always sufficient for me, but He loved me enough to keep me in place until He determined I was ready for authentication. Psalm 138:8, The Lord will perfect that which concerns me, comes to mind as I write this chapter, because that's exactly what He did in this season. When it was all over, He lovingly wrapped up all I experienced through cutting and polishing and used the diamond's 5C grading process to reveal His finished work in me.

Five C's of Diamond Grading

The process of diamond grading has typically consisted of 4 C's: Carat, Color, Clarity, and Cut; however, there's a fifth C: Certification.[2] This phase investigates the integrity of the diamond. It answers the questions, "How effective was the cutting and polishing process? Is it ready for public presentation? Is it worth the jeweler's asking price?"

---

2   "The 5 C's of Diamonds (Yes, 5): The Diamond Details You Don't Want to Miss."*Naturaldiamonds.Com*, 15 May 2025, www.naturaldiamonds.com/engagement-rings/5-cs-diamonds-guide/. Accessed 29 Jul. 2025.

The Lord used the diamond's 5C grading process to reveal the results that cutting and polishing had in my life. Let's look at them in greater detail and understand what they mean to us spiritually.

Carat

The term carat is often misunderstood.[3] It refers to a diamond's weight, not its size. A high-carat-weight diamond with a poor cut may look smaller than a diamond with a smaller carat weight and a very good cut. I learned that most people misplace their emphasis when shopping for a diamond. They believe the higher the carat, the more valuable the diamond, when in fact it's the cut that determines value, not carat. The better the cut, the more the diamond will sparkle.[4]

What does carat mean for us spiritually? It means everything because though it isn't the most important element in selecting a diamond, from a spiritual perspective, carat is uber important. It's what impacts the people we encounter. It's the weight of God's glory on our lives. The weightier the glory, the greater the impact and the greater the promotion. The weight of God's glory on our lives causes us to reflect His characteristics, but it only comes after we have endured various trials of pressure that cut away our flesh and let Him in. It is only then that His presence sits down in our lives and we find ourselves responding like Him.

Refusal to repay people when they hurt us, no matter how badly, is an example of God's glory working through us. The glory of God at work won't allow us to harbor bitterness. It won't allow us to succumb to the

---

3 "The 4 C's of Diamonds: Evaluating Diamond Quality." *Diamonds.Pro*, 9 Jun. 2025 (Updated), www.diamonds.pro/education/4cs-diamonds/. Accessed 5 May 2024.
4 [YouTube (Posted Originally by CNNMoney)]. (2024, May 5). See How Diamonds are Cut from Rocks [Video]. YouTube (Posted Originally by CNNMoney).

enemy's trick to push us to the place where we get outside of character. Instead, we maintain who we are. We show mercy instead of vengeance and love instead of hate. We give this to others because this is what God gives to us.

There have been many occasions when the Lord allowed people to misuse and abuse me. The experiences seemed to come one after the other, but with each lesson came transformation. Robin before the cutting and polishing process repaid evil for evil, but Robin after the cutting and polishing process learned how to be still and let God be God. I trusted Him enough to bite my tongue and tell my flesh, "Sit down. No, you will not respond." Beloved, this is when the weight of God's glory began to show up in my life. That's when, like the diamond, God's weight in my life made me a valuable tool in His kingdom because He could trust me and use me to bless His people.

Remain Humble

One thing to remember when God's weight rests upon us is to remain humble. The weight of His presence produces some amazing fruit, like miracles, signs, and wonders (Hebrews 2:4). If we aren't careful, we might think it's us and not Him.

I recall a time when I ran into a former church member who had just lost her mother. I asked her how she was doing, and she responded with a quick, "Fine," and walked away. Holy Spirit said, "She's not fine. Go to her." Tears streamed down her face by the time I caught up with her. I took her hands and prayed, and immediately the healing oil of God began to flow. Healing and deliverance took place at that moment. Beloved, this experience encouraged me. It let me know my suffering was not in vain and that my painful tests were being used as a footstool for elevation. Glory be to God!

Color

Grading a diamond for its color refers to the diamond's lack of color.[5] The clearer the diamond, the higher the value. However, for the sake of Perfection, I will focus on diamond color as it relates to the more fancy, colorful diamonds. Those rare and costly gems with deep saturations of color make them unique and extremely valuable. These diamonds come in all colors of the rainbow, but I will pay particular attention to blue, green, yellow/gold, and circle back around to the colorless diamond.

Looking at diamond colors through a spiritual lens reveals that colors, like numbers, have significant biblical meaning. Understanding what different colors symbolize can help us gain a deeper revelation in our faith walk.[6]

God used colors during this season to reveal what He was accomplishing in me. I believe He wanted to encourage me to stay the course because the cutting process was so painful. The following colors represent what God spoke to my spirit during this season:

Blue – God used blue to reveal Holy Spirit was at work in me. He revealed that healing was taking place, I was not alone, and that His peace was with me. I'd notice different people wearing various shades of blue that caught my attention, or a blue car would cut me off while driving. Things like

---

5   "The 4 C's of Diamonds: What's Important When Buying Diamonds?" *Naturallycolored.Com*, www.naturallycolored.com/diamond-education/diamond-grading/4cs-of-diamonds. Accessed 5 May 2024.

6   "Is There Any Significance to Colors in the Bible?" *Christianity.com*. Accessed September 13, 2024

this happened throughout this season of my life as the Lord sought to drive home the point that Holy Spirit was at work in me.

Green - God highlighted green to teach me I was growing in Him and that He was bringing wealth, prosperity, renewal, resurrection, restoration, and newness of life to me. Unlike blue, the Lord revealed what green represented through a demonstration I won't soon forget.

One day, a woman entered my salon and inquired about my services. She stopped in mid-sentence as she spoke and said, "I see money all around you." She said she couldn't say what she saw, she had to show me, and went into her purse and pulled out five, ten, and twenty-dollar bills and rained them over my head! She fell to the floor under the power of Holy Spirit once she finished. I stood frozen in amazement as I watched this woman demonstrate the very words the Lord spoke to my spirit. She was sent by God to perform openly what He communicated to me through the color green. God highlighted this color at just about any moment of my life. I could be watching TV, at work, or out and about-it didn't matter. God wanted to make sure I understood what He was saying through green.

Yellow/Gold - Gold is indicative of change, the glory, anointing, faith, joy, presence of God, holiness, divine nature, majesty, wealth, success and status, wisdom, knowledge, understanding, and enlightenment. God sent prophets to confirm what He communicated through this color. Some of them I knew, others I didn't, but they all prophesied the same message: God would prepare a table of blessings before me in the presence of my enemies. In the natural, people who misused and abused me would come to my salon and ask if they could work there. They had no place else to go but back to me. Surrounded by gold walls, the presence of the Lord, and the blessing that was upon my life, they knew they could return because they'd be safe, and they were right. God used the blessing of my salon to provide a safe place for those who thought they were abusing me to work. What they didn't know is that their abuse became my blessing of elevation. To God be the glory!

I'd also see coins (nickels and dimes) on the ground in various places during this time, which represents grace and change. Strangers approached me in public to tell me I would be wealthy one day. Wealth shined through me, and God allowed people to see it. Beloved, it was an exciting time.

Clear/Colorless – Clear is synonymous with Holy Spirit, purifying the soul, admission into the faith, brightness, cleanliness, purity in the sight of God, justified, being regarded as just, made innocent, cleansed, and translucence.

God certainly knows how to mix things up at the precise moment we think we have Him figured out. He used a woman who refused to pay me after I serviced her to highlight the meaning of this color and all that it meant. I'd worked on her for hours, and she accumulated a significant tab by the time I was finished. Beloved, she looked in the mirror and told me she wouldn't pay her bill in full because she didn't have enough money. Then she proceeded to tell me she wasn't happy with her hair anyway. My flesh boiled as I listened to her. She knew my work. She wasn't a new client. I grew angrier by the minute. I wrestled with my flesh, prayed, and wrestled with my flesh some more to hold my peace. I finally told her to have a nice day when I realized she wasn't going to pay me. It was painful. God used my coworkers to affirm His work in me after she left. They told me I was a true woman of God who was pure in heart. Beloved, it wasn't that I didn't want to react. I chose not to react, and as a result, God was glorified.

God used each of these colors to illuminate the work He accomplished in me. He did not allow me to hear His voice; instead, He trained me to hear Him through colors.

Clarity

The fewer visible imperfections a diamond has, the higher its diamond clarity rating.[7] They are studied for flaws that are referred to as surface flaws or blemishes, and internal defects known as inclusions. Diamond Clarity is an important characteristic that affects a diamond's beauty. Likewise, the Lord used the Clarity grading process to highlight any remaining flaws and imperfections in me. The lingering, often small, and seemingly insignificant things that prevent Him from receiving maximum glory from our lives.

Allow me to open this segment with an experience that occurred well before my season of cutting and polishing. I'll preface this by saying I was in my 20s. I was in a relationship with the Lord but not yet sanctified.

One day, I took a short break between clients to get something to eat at a nearby sandwich shop with my best friend. I overheard the worker talking rudely to Chelsea as she tried to order, like unnecessarily rude. Now, I wasn't the type of person to go off on people for no reason unless

---

7   (n.d.) Flawless Diamonds: Education and FAQ (includes explanation of diamond clarity and grading). Bluenile.com.

they messed with someone I loved, then I lost it. This was one of those moments. Beloved, I told the worker about herself and colored it with some choice words. It was bad. When I was finished, I heard, "Hey Reverend Wilson, you cussin' now?" The words came from a member of the church I attended. "What?" I said to myself. I could've hit the floor. God said, "See, you never know whose watching." It was the perfect setup to teach me a valuable lesson and reveal my flaws. He'll do it every time.

Twenty years later the Lord revealed my level of Clarity through a quick, but painful accident at work. My client and I were having a wonderful time chatting it up while I pressed her hair. I became distracted at some point in the conversation and reached for the pressing comb that was cooling off on a towel. I laid my hand down to rest it upon what I thought was the towel, and it rested flat on the hot comb. It was so hot I heard my hand sizzle. I quickly snatched it away and yelled, "Ouch!" That was it. A co-worker approached me later that day and shared that she saw and heard me when I burned my hand. She told me that experience showed her who I was at my core, because in moments like those there's no time to apply a filter. She told me I was a true woman of God. Beloved, let me tell you, God did that!

Cut

The cut of a diamond significantly influences its brilliance. A well-cut diamond reflects light internally from one facet to another and disperses it through the top of the stone, resulting in exceptional sparkle.[8] Will it be round, heart-shaped, oval, marquise, or pear? It's up to the gemologist

---

8 "The 5 C's of Diamonds (Yes, 5): The Diamond Details You Don't Want to Miss." *Naturaldiamonds. Com*, 15 May 2025, www.naturaldiamonds.com/engagement-rings/5-cs-diamonds-guide/. Accessed 29 Jul. 2025.

whose job is to choose the shape that will yield the highest quality and the most money from the rough stone.

Beloved, the Lord made us and not we ourselves. He is intimately acquainted with all our ways. He knows what He put in us from the beginning of time, and, like the gemologist, He is the expert on how He desires to use our processes to shape us for a specific use. Are we a pastor, a prophet, an evangelist, a singer, a songwriter, a businessperson? The Lord, our Holy gemologist, uses the cutting and polishing process to shape us for whatever purpose He's placed in us.

Beloved, the Lord allowed various trials to cut away the unnecessary residue that clung to me and dulled His brilliance in my life. He cut away fears, spiritual shackles, relationships, attitudes, dispositions, mindsets, and behaviors. Those fleshly attributes that were of no use to the person of the spirit, so the diamond He created before time began could burst forth. The more things were cut away from me the brighter I shined.

One day the Lord used a painfully embarrassing incident to prepare me to walk into the office of a Preacher. A woman asked me to serve as guest speaker at her church. The day of the service began like every other day. Nothing unusual occurred, and there were no signs of an impending spiritual hindrance, but a blanket of fear swept over me as I approached the podium and looked over the audience. My mind went completely blank, and my body froze. I stammered uncontrollably as I looked into the eyes of the audience. I stood before the people in the natural, but spiritually I wrestled with the demonic spirit of fear that had me arrested and ineffective.

So many thoughts bombarded my mind in that moment. I feared the people's judgment. I feared I wasn't educated enough and that perhaps

God had the wrong person in mind when He chose me. You see, when you are chosen, the enemy plans his attacks early in life. I was stricken with a disease as a child and completely lost my short-term memory. I had to relearn how to read and write. As a result, I struggled with confidence to effectively communicate with people. Fear told me everyone who looked at me knew my story.

Well, needless to say I did a horrible job. And, here's the kicker, my subject was on breaking spiritual chains! It was so bad it wasn't worthy of the obligatory applause I received. The woman who invited me didn't give me the love offering she had for me. She thanked me, envelope with the love offering in hand, but the envelope did not see my hands. Fear won that battle, but God worked it out so that it would be the last time it oppressed me.

I went home that afternoon defeated and embarrassed, but God used that experience to prime me for a great deliverance years later that happened so unassumingly.

I tuned in to a program one Sunday afternoon that aired a sermon by Sarah Jakes. Not only was her message on point, but she spoke with so much confidence, power, and authority that it caught my attention. "That's you," the Lord said. I thought for a moment and said, "Really, God? If that's me, then that means I can do this. I can speak and not tremble." Beloved, I *believed* the Lord's words and, just like that, the fear of public speaking was broken. It was a quick, yet powerful moment of deliverance that forever changed the way I saw myself and my ability to stand before God's people and preach His Word. Today I walk boldly and effectively in the five-fold ascension gifts for the building up of the body of Christ. Praise His Name!

Certification

Certification is what anchors the other four C's in truth. A diamond may appear brilliant or flawless, but without a trusted grading report, you're buying on assumption.[9] This process authenticates the diamond just before it is presented to the public for sale.

The Lord uses this phase to show His children and others around them what He accomplished in them. It's His way of saying, "Look at what I did!" to the world and to us. I just love Him! I'll close this chapter with a short, funny story as to how the Lord used the Certification process to reveal what He perfected in me.

I took pictures to prepare for the release of my first book. The photographer called me frustrated and said, "Robin, the pictures are done, but you have this glow all around you that I can't seem to get out. I've done everything, and nothing works!" "Boy, that's the glory of God on me. You can't take out the glory, just let it stay," I said without missing a beat. No editing program the photographer used could remove the glow that surrounded me. The Lord would not allow it. He wanted the world to see His accomplishment. Just like a diamond is held up for inspection during the Certification inspection, I believe in this moment the Lord held me up and said, "Process complete. This area of her life is perfected, and she's ready to move closer to Purpose." Glory be to God!

---

9   "The 5 C's of Diamonds (Yes, 5): The Diamond Details You Don't Want to Miss." *Naturaldiamonds. Com*, 15 May 2025, www.naturaldiamonds.com/engagement-rings/5-cs-diamonds-guide/. Accessed 29 Jul. 2025.

Key Points

- You are God's diamond
- God uses colors to speak to us to let us know what He is up to in our lives
- Remember to remain humble when God's glory begins to manifest in your life
- God is like a Holy gemologist. He is the expert on how He desires to use our processes to shape us for a specific use

In Your Quiet Time

Beloved, remember you are a beautiful, precious diamond who God is preparing to present to the world. Like the preciousness of a diamond, you are precious in the sight of the Lord—His best for the earth. He's preparing to present you and the gifts He's placed in you to bless His people. If you find yourself experiencing any of the 5C's, please remain in the process until the Lord has accomplished His work in and through you. The results will be brilliant.

1. What stage of the 5C grading process are you in?
2. How does it make you feel when the Lord reveals the beautiful things He's accomplished in you?
3. Recalling what you read about Cut, how has the Lord shaped you? Pray and ask Holy Spirit to mightily use you in this area as you fully embrace your shape.

CHAPTER 7:

PREPARING FOR PURPOSE

Out on a Limb for God

"When God asks, 'Are you ready for purpose?' He wants to know if you are ready for what you are about to encounter for His sake. The rejection, the laughs, the taunts, and the slander. He wants to know if you are ready to choose humility over pride, and obedience over comfort."

-ROBIN RENEE

When I heard the words, "Are you ready?" I knew Purpose was calling. It was a very comfortable time. My husband and I co-taught a class, and I taught Sunday school. My clientele was booming. My girls were excelling in school. Life was great according to the world's standards, but I was dying spiritually. I was not truly walking in my spiritual gifts the way God desired. Part of Him asking the question, "Are you ready?"

was preparation for what He was about to do to me, in me, and through me for Purpose's sake. He saw how comfortable I was and desired to shake things up.

On one occasion, a dear friend of mine asked me to pray at a women's conference where she was the guest speaker. That Saturday morning of the conference, God said, "Today I will **expose** you." I said, "**Expose** me? God, if you're exposing me, that means I'm hidden." That revelation was eye-opening, and I tell you that day, God did exactly what He said He would do. He mightily exposed the gifts and anointings He placed in me. I prophesied, laid hands, and people were healed, delivered, and baptized in the Spirit. I was like a rushing wave unleashed upon the people of God, and He got all the glory. People who'd known me for years saw something come out of me they never saw before. Some embraced it and understood it as a supernatural move of God through me. Others said I was being in-fluenced by Satan, and I operated through witchcraft. I remember seeing a fellow church leader after the service, and she ignored me as if I were invisible. That hurt me to my core because we always had a good relation-ship. God used that experience to teach me that when you are surrendered to Him, people will not always understand, and you may offend some in obeying Him. 1Corinthians 2:14 says, But the natural man does not re-ceive the things of the Spirit of God, for they are foolishness to him; nor can he know them, because they are spiritually discerned.

God reinforced the fact that He, alone, was training and developing me for Purpose. It is both beautiful and lonely when you are hand-selected and trained by God. Beautiful in that the things He teaches you come straight from Him and are accompanied with so much life-changing pow-er, but it is also lonely in that not everyone understands the power of God and the ways of God. Sometimes, He'll have you do things that put you directly at odds with people who are not on the inside of what He is doing in your life, and this has the potential to perpetuate a cycle of rejection.

Out on a Limb for Purpose

I was asked to pray for a woman who was possessed by demons after a Sunday morning church service. It didn't take long for Holy Spirit to begin moving. Progress was being made. Many spirits were cast out of her, and we were just on the brink of a pivotal breaking point when I received word that time was up and we had to leave the church grounds. I couldn't believe my ears. I stopped out of obedience, and as a result, I had to leave this woman's spirit open and vulnerable to other spirits entering or old ones returning. It was heartbreaking because her life could have been completely changed in that encounter. I knew then I could not engage in spiritual warfare prayers on that level under that spiritual authority because I couldn't be sure I would have the time needed to complete the deliverance. The Lord showed me in that moment who I was in Him, what He'd placed in me, and that I would not remain where I was for long.

The second time I found myself out on a limb for Purpose was during a church service, and the Holy Spirit fell upon me. I began to speak in an unknown tongue that required interpretation. This was unorthodox for a Baptist church, so I knew there had to be an interpreter if the Lord released the tongues. I anxiously waited for someone to come forth, but no one came. I was shocked. A fellow pastor approached me after service and told me she had the interpretation. "What?" I said. "I can't believe you had me out there and didn't give the interpretation God gave you. He could've received great glory." Beloved, God wanted to use that moment to supersede tradition and ritualistic worship. He wanted to reveal Himself in a deeper capacity to the church. He wanted them to see a power they'd never seen before. God continued exposing me, and I continued experiencing rejection, but a prophet is not without honor except in his own country and in his own house (Matthew 13:57).

Beloved, I feel it is important to tell you I respect spiritual authority. I would never do anything in a church that the pastor of that house forbids. I believe the Lord would lead me to leave a church before I offended and disrespected the leadership of that house. The tongues I experienced were like the ones on the day of Pentecost. Like the tongues that fell upon the apostles and they spoke as the Spirit gave them utterance, those were the tongues that fell upon me, and I spoke as the Spirit gave me utterance. I knew God provided an interpretation because He's a God of order, and I also knew that 1 Corinthians 14:27 says, if anyone speaks in a tongue, let there be two or at the most three, each in turn, and let one interpret. I was the one, and my fellow prophet was the second. Because the interpretation did not come forth, I, once again, found myself out on a limb for God and vulnerable to the criticisms of man.

God later led me to start a home bible study where I believe He fine-tuned my gifts and brought me closer to my Purpose. He trained and developed me in spiritual warfare, healing, and deliverance. I also gained wisdom as to when to seek spiritual help to handle cases that were not mine to handle. For example, there was an occasion when a woman came to my salon seeking deliverance who was pregnant with demons. I could audibly hear them speaking. I knew I had the power and authority to cast them out, but I recognized the time was not right. I knew demons could jump from one person to another and could really put on a show when they are being cast out, and I did not want to use my salon as a stage for Satan. I told the woman I was going to have to refer her to my spiritual father. Praise be to God, He exercised His God-given authority and drove them out of the woman.

Beloved, walking in Purpose isn't always convenient, it doesn't always feel good, and you will have to walk alone, but know that if God has called you to Purpose, He will equip you for Purpose. Yes, the lessons will come, but don't worry because they come to train and validate you. It's in you to fulfill everything the Lord has called you to do because He's already equipped and qualified you (Romans 8:30). Just know this: The safest place, though tumultuous at times, is the place of Purpose. Remain there.

Key Points
- A prophet is not recognized in their own home
- When you are surrendered to God, people will not always understand
- You may offend some in the process of being obedient
- God will have you do things that put you directly at odds with people who are not on the inside of what He is doing in your life
- When God exposes you, He shows you and others who you truly are
- The safest place, though tumultuous at times, is the place of Purpose

In Your Quiet Time
Are you currently experiencing rejection because of Purpose? Are you dealing with men and women of God who are not on the inside of what God is doing in your life?

If your answer is yes, I invite you to recite the following prayer:

Dear Lord,

Thank you for calling me and choosing me for Purpose. Father, I ask that You help me choose You and Your will over comfort and the approval of man. Thank You that in Jesus Christ I am bold and courageous. Thank You that no matter what level of rejection I experience for You, I will endure and remain in peace (shalom). In Jesus' Name, Amen.

CHAPTER 8:

PAIN

It was Good that I was Afflicted

So we're not giving up. How could we! Even though on the outside it often looks like things are falling apart on us, on the inside, where God is making new life, not a day goes by without His unfolding grace. These hard times are small potatoes compared to the coming good times, the lavish celebration prepared for us. There's far more here than meets the eye. The things we see now are here today, gone tomorrow. But the things we can't see now will last forever.

2 CORINTHIANS 4:16-18, THE MESSAGE VERSION

I can't think of one person in this world who can say they like pain. That wouldn't be natural. It hurts and is very uncomfortable. But, with all the discomfort that it brings, pain has the uncanny ability to bring about the most significant change in a person's life. It can also be the catalyst that releases some of the biggest blessings-you know, the kind that come in and overtake you.

I love the Message version of 2 Corinthians 4:16-18. Listen to what it says: So we're not giving up. How could we! Even though on the outside it often looks like things are falling apart on us, on the inside, where God is making new life, not a day goes by without his unfolding grace. These hard times are small potatoes compared to the coming good times, the lavish celebration prepared for us. There's far more here than meets the eye. The things we see now are here today, gone tomorrow. But the things we can't see now will last forever.

Beloved, that's it. That's what it's all about. Going through the pain so we can come out on the other side with a far greater weight of glory. That is exactly what God was doing in me as I journeyed through a painful season of life towards glory. Let me share my story.

My Mother

My first experience in this season was with the loss of my beloved mother, Rosalea Robinson. More than a mother. She was my confidant, my right arm, a God-fearing prophet, my loudest cheerleader, and my most honest critic. I knew I could count on her for anything and everything I needed. Her love was undeniable. My mother loved fiercely. She was going to tell you in her own Rosalea Robinson way, and she was going to show you with her actions.

God knew the exact type of mom I needed. She encouraged me to conquer my fears, and her influence in my life ran deep. She instilled a deep sense of faith in me that will last a lifetime. I was devastated when I learned she had cancer. I couldn't imagine life without her. I had already lost my sister and my father, and with the threat of my mom leaving me, it was a lot for me to handle.

It goes without saying that I knew God could heal my mother in an instant from her cancer. It also goes without saying that God has, on numerous occasions, healed many people through me. With these two things ringing true, it was so ironic that God never once led me to pray for her healing. Not once did He instruct me to lay hands on her, and not once did I ever do it. As much as I wanted to see my mom get up from her bed of affliction, my obedience to the Lord outweighed my personal desire. Don't get me wrong, my ears, mouth, and hands were always in the ready position in case He decided to give me the instruction. All I needed was to hear from Him, and the words, prayers, and laying of hands were as good as done. I waited with anticipation but never received instructions. It was difficult, but I chose to trust God.

My mom suffered throughout the time she battled cancer. It was hard for me to watch, but what was hardest was that I couldn't be by her side. My life and ministry still had to go on. I still had bills to pay, clients who depended on me, and my husband and home still needed my attention. The demands of my life collided with my desire to be with my mom every waking moment, and it didn't feel good. All the while, God was telling me to keep going. To keep showing up for work, to continue with ministry, to be there for my family, and that He had my mother.

While I listened and obeyed, it was still rough because I began to see the dynamic of our relationship change before my eyes. The once quick-witted, funny, bubbly person I always knew wasn't the same. I wasn't able to lean on her the way I was used to. I couldn't pick up the phone and burden her with my stuff because she was dealing with something much bigger.

In hindsight, I could see how God was prepping me to lean on Him and Him alone. His mercy allowed this process to happen over time, giving me time to reset and get used to the idea that my mom was no longer available for me the way she had always been.

The passing of time allowed me to adjust to living life with my mom's new role in my life. I was ok with her new role because that meant she was still here. In my mind, I still had my mommy on this side of heaven, but the reality was she was suffering. I remember one day my aunt told me I needed to release her because she was okay with transitioning. In fact, she wanted to transition but was holding on because she knew I wasn't ready to release her, and she was right. I wasn't ready.

As I sat by her bedside one day I heard her call out, "Am I still here? Am I dead yet?" We told her she was still here, and I'll never forget her response. She was disappointed. At that moment, it hit me like a ton of bricks. My mom was tired of fighting, and I was operating selfishly by refusing to let her go. I asked God to forgive me and to give me the strength to allow her to transition. It was just days later that I had peace in releasing my mom, and I told her that. I told her I was okay with her leaving. That it was okay to go. The moment I did that, her process of transition sped up rapidly.

The day my mom transitioned was the day I instinctively knew I didn't have anyone else to lean on the way I leaned on her. From big to small and everything in between, I would have to lean on God. Her departure left an empty void in me, but it gave God more of me to fill, and believe me, He did just that.

My Business

When God gave me my first shop, it was a dream come true. When He gave me my second shop, it was the fulfillment of His promise to me. And, I must say He showed OUT as He brought it to pass. His powerful right hand was evident in so many ways that those who watched it happen agreed with me that it was only God who gifted me with Trinity Experience Salon. It took my faith to a whole new level. Sometimes people who didn't know my story would ask me how I got the shop, and all I would say is, "It's the favor of God." And it truly was His beautiful hand of favor in my life that gave me Trinity Experience Salon.

The beginning of this experience was lovely. My salon was gorgeous— all my booths were filled, and I was doing very well financially. I enjoyed the fruits of Trinity for about 11 years, then one day God decided He wanted to do something fresh and new in my life—enter COVID-19. The entrance of COVID changed everything for so many people, and I am no different.

God told me He wanted to give me something new. The release of that word in my life was the beginning of things falling apart. My business, from customers to booth renters, began to dry up seemingly overnight, but the bills still needed to be paid. As I said earlier in the book, everyone around me was getting loans except me. God continued to tell me He would be my source and to be content. He was going to provide for me, and He did. So, when the time came to let go of the salon, it was very difficult. I fought hard to save it. I prayed and believed God for provision, but it was always just enough to pay my rent. Not enough to take me over. God, in His grace, knew how hard it was for me to let go. Much like holding on to my mom and not wanting to release her, Trinity Experience Salon was my promise, and I didn't want to let it go. It was my evidence of what God could do. But He wanted to do more, and He simply needed me to release what was in my hand so that He could give me more.

As simple as that sounds, it wasn't. Trinity defined me, and I thought I'd entered my promised land with this blessing. I wouldn't find out until after I let it go that Trinity was actually my wilderness season, where God would train and prepare me for what He had waiting for me. The Lord began to tell me that it was my training ground and preparation for where He was taking me the moment I embraced the idea of releasing the salon. I had to let it go because my training was coming to an end. With Trinity, I saw that God could do big things, and that He was a supernatural Provider and Keeper. It also prepared me for the ministry work He would have me do. Yes, Trinity Experience was a hair salon, but can I tell you that in that hair salon I learned how to do battle and overcome personalities, snakes, Leviathan spirits, different witches and warlocks, and Jezebel spirits. I was visited by angels, demons tried to take up residence in my shop, a woman tried to take my shop from under me, and the list goes on. Beloved, it was real. Each time I mastered a test, another one would immediately follow. Looking at Trinity through that lens helped me to release it completely.

Beloved, it is impossible to beat God at giving. Earlier, I said I had to release Trinity so that God could give me what He had for me. Well, not only did God provide me with another salon, He also blessed me with a podcast, a Christian clothing line, and I am receiving more ministry opportunities through conferences and workshops, and people are being blessed. To God be the glory!

My Best Friend

If I didn't understand that God was serious about me leaning on Him and Him alone, that message came across loud and clear the day my best friend of 30 years told me she was relocating to another state. My mom always told me that if I found one person I considered my friend, I should count myself blessed. Well, I found that person in Chelsea. She's my travel partner, my children's Godmother, my shopping buddy, my sister, and my ministry helper. Beloved, my heart literally sank with the news. She, like my mother, father, and sister (all of whom God moved), was being taken as well. Praise God, it was only to another state, but like all the others who had to go, she, too, was being removed from my life in the way she had been for so many years. Though stunned by the news, deep down I wasn't surprised. God was serious about what He was doing in my life. I had no other choice but to embrace her family's move to another state, and that broke my heart. Who was I going to talk to now? Who was I going to vent to? Go shopping with? Lean on to do this or that? Help me in ministry? Who was I going to be able to let my guard down around? The answer was God to each of these questions. Just like He stepped in and filled the void of my mother, He stepped in and filled the void of my best friend moving away. He was literally filling yet another empty space with Himself.

Myself

As I traveled through this season, experiencing one loss after another, God allowed me to see myself. Every loss opened my eyes to the inner Robin. I got to see myself and what was inside of me as I grappled with the losses. Busyness became my coping mechanism. As I self-reflect, I see myself relating to Martha from the Gospel of Luke 10:38-42. Martha, busy serving and distracted by her tasks, embodies the struggles I faced. While she worked diligently to welcome Jesus into her home, she became overwhelmed and frustrated. It wasn't until Jesus gently reminded her that Mary had chosen the better portion-sitting at his feet that I began to see my own life reflected in her story. Like Martha, I was caught in a whirl-wind of responsibilities. I kept myself busy, thinking that if I stayed active, I could outrun my grief. My distractions prevented me from truly walking in my purpose. I lost my identity in all my grief and busyness, so I had to do some soul searching.

This was my turning point; I took some time for myself, and I realized that I didn't like who I had become. I realized I had been avoiding my pain rather than facing it. The busyness I embraced was a shield that pre-vented me from confronting my sorrows. This moment of clarity led me to reflect on Mary, who chose to sit at Jesus's feet, absorbing his teachings and presence. After reevaluating myself and understanding that to heal, I needed to transition from a distracted Martha to a devoted Mary, I began to sit at God's feet.

A shift happened the minute I carved out more time to dwell in His presence. I immersed myself in prayer and scripture, allowing His pres-ence to envelop me. Psalm 46:10 resonated deeply within my spirit, Be Still and know that I am God. I discovered the power of rest and reflection in those quiet moments. A sense of warmth, comfort, and understanding washed over me as I continued to read my bible and pray. My pain didn't disappear, but it began to transform. I experienced healing through the simple act of sitting at the feet of Jesus, allowing His love to fill the empty spaces in my heart.

The actions of both Martha and Mary play important roles in our spiritual lives. Martha's service is essential, but it must be rooted in devotion to God. Finding balance is crucial; we cannot pour from an empty cup. In addition to that, we must know that walking in our purpose is not an easy task and requires us to spend time at the feet of Jesus and be ready and willing to release what He requires us to release.

When God is calling you to purpose, you cannot be distracted by the things around you, nor can you take your old mindset with you (worry, fear, and uncertainty, to name a few). God has elevated me from my old mindset, and it came through sitting at His feet and maintaining the proper posture of worship and resting in Him. Throughout this period, Matthew 11: 28-29 became my rock scripture: Come to me, all you who are weary and burdened, and I will give you rest. To God be the glory!

Key Points

- God will remove people you've always depended upon so that He can be your only source of support
- It is impossible to beat God at giving
- Finding balance is crucial; we cannot pour from an empty cup
- When God is calling you to purpose, you cannot be distracted by the things around you

In Your Quiet Time

Find a quiet place where you can be still in the presence of God. Your quiet place can be your car, your backyard, your prayer room, or on a walk. Practice listening and dwelling in His presence. Show up without your agenda and allow the Lord's presence to come in and envelope you. It's in the quiet stillness that restoration can happen.

CHAPTER 9:

PROMOTION

Welcome to Purpose

"Without God, life has no purpose, and without purpose, life has no meaning. Without meaning, life has no significance or hope."

–Rick Warren

The Lord finally spoke those three words I longed to hear: "You are Ready." These words meant all the hard lessons and trials I experienced brought me to this very moment. I was finally in a place where He could mightily use me. I was honored.

When God speaks, expect change. My ministry went to a completely new level in anointing and power after He spoke, "You are ready." The power I operated in prior to this announcement was nothing compared to the power I walk in today.

The Lord told me I was called to wreck regions, I was called to the marketplace, that I would have a ministry like His for so many years. For years, I longed to see His words come to pass. Year after year I thought it would be my time, only to discover I was entering yet another phase of refinement. This time, Beloved, rather than introducing me to another test or trial, He set me up to show me what was in me and that, yes, I was ready indeed.

Fortified to Fight

The definition of fortified means to be made stronger or more secure; to protect or strengthen against attack. God showed me I was fortified through an experience with a booth renter who was possessed by demonic spirits. I knew something wasn't right when she entered and said, "I'm here for you." This woman brought so much discord to my salon. She intimidated my booth renters and my clients. Doors opened and closed on their own at any given moment.

One morning, I had a dream that I crushed the head of a huge serpent with the heel of my shoe, then I heard the Lord say, "I have given you authority to defeat Leviathan." I felt so much warfare concerning my life and the salon as I got out of bed. I told my girlfriend it was time for those spirits to leave my business, as I poured my heart out to her about what I experienced.

The door opened on its own as I approached the salon. "I saw that," the woman said as I entered. God was letting that spirit in her know I was fortified by Him and protected by His angels. The warfare increased as the day progressed. The looks, snide remarks, and trance-like states were too much to have to deal with. I called my spiritual mother at one point to ask for help in casting the spirits out of the salon, to which she responded, "The same way you let them in is the same way you kick them out." She was not coming. I needed to handle this one on my own. The dream I had that morning reminded me that I had victory, so I told the young lady I needed to talk to her outside. In short, I told her she had to go. I feel it is important to share that I invited this woman to Bible study on many occasions to experience the healing and deliverance she needed, but she declined every one of my offers. In hindsight, I believe God sent her to my salon to receive a blessing and to show me who I was in Him; however, she refused to yield to the power of God and accept what He had for her.

I told the woman she had to leave, and she did. She didn't put up a fight, and the spirits in her knew their time was up. She left quietly but still possessed. Beloved, God used that situation to let me know He fortified me and that I was spiritually equipped to handle situations like that. To God be the glory, He showed me through this situation that being ready meant I was ready to handle whatever came my way.

Miracles, Signs, and Wonders

A woman came into my prayer line on one occasion. The Lord instructed me to lay my hands on her face and pray for her. After it was over, she told me the Lord restored feeling on the side of her face the moment I touched her. She'd been suffering from paralysis for several years. I had no idea what she was suffering from, but God knew, and He used me to bring the miracle of healing to her life.

On another occasion, I prayed for my spiritual mom whose face was twisted from a stroke. As I prayed, the Lord healed her right before our eyes. Her mouth, which was once twisted, was immediately brought back into alignment. To God be the glory!

Beloved, I experienced great victories in healing and deliverance, and at the same time Ephesians 6:11, Put on the whole armor of God, that you may be able to stand against the wiles of the devil, became increasingly personal in my life. Just as the anointing in my life increased, so did the level of spiritual opposition. It was another realm of spiritual warfare. It was no longer me fighting against evil spirits in people. I became the assignment of principalities and spirits in high places. The Lord prepared me for this moment by letting me know that for every new level, there will be a new devil, but turning back is never an option. I knew the power of God, and I also knew His power lived in me.

Everything changed for me. Things *had* to change. Why? Because you can't go into a new season doing old things, operating in old ways. Mark 2:22 says, And no one puts new wine into old wineskins; or else the new wine bursts the wineskins, the wine is spilled, and the wineskins are ruined. But new wine must be put into new wineskins. Every lesson, every trial, and every process prepared me to operate in Purpose.

Beloved, those three words spoken by the Lord ushered me into Purpose in every area of my life. All my businesses began to thrive, the Lord opened the door for me to start my podcast, He sent people to work for me, I saw financial increase, and I began walking in a new level of favor with men and women I'd never experienced before.

The Lord told me He was smiling at me at one point. When I asked Him to explain who else in the Bible he smiled at, He told me David, Paul, Joseph, and Esther. He revealed that He smiled at them because they persevered through fiery trials in pursuit of His purpose for their lives. He said He smiled at them because they trusted Him. Each one of these individuals had to leave a place of comfort in pursuit of God's plan of Purpose. They went through fiery, scary trials filled with persecution, but they stayed the course.

The Lord ended our conversation by telling me He'd changed my name to Esther, which means shining star. Would you believe that not many days later, people began telling me they saw me as a queen, and I took them from dark places because I carried a light? I don't say this to brag. I give all glory to God because none of this was my doing. I was a hot mess before God got His hands on me. It was only by His grace and mercy and His call upon my life that I am who I am.

Key Points
· For every new level (promotion), there is a new devil
· You can't go into Promotion doing old things
· Everything must change to accommodate the person you have become
· Welcome to Purpose

In Your Quiet Time
The Lord's word to you is, "You are Ready." You are polished and you radiate His glory. Enter your Purpose, a place where lack of any kind will no longer hinder you. A place where He provides every connection and every resource you need. A place of open doors and torn-down walls, and a place where no demon or principality will ever stop you. Congratulations on your promotion, Beloved, and welcome to Purpose!

A CLOSING PRAYER

Blessings Beloved,

I am so honored you allowed me to speak into your life through this book. I know your season of stretching was not easy. I know there were times you felt like you were going to break, but the Lord did not allow it. His Spirit in you allowed you to endure to the very end, and now you are ready to walk in your true destiny as a game changer, to shake the nations, and to wreck regions for the Kingdom of God.

May the favor of God rest upon your life as He draws you closer and deeper into the things He has purposed for you. May you experience a deeper relationship with Him that empowers you to run the race He has set before you. My Beloved, your destiny is great, and you are ready to experience a mighty move from our God. May the Holy Spirit fill you with all power as you move forward.

In the name of Jesus, Amen.

THE MINISTRY OF NUMBERS

"God is quietly speaking through numbers. Numbers are a Biblical means God speaks to His people. For those sensitive to 'See' with prophetic vision what God is revealing, are hearing His voice loudly."

DESTINY EASTGATE MINISTRIES

I would be remiss if I did not talk about how the Lord used numbers to usher me into His divine plan for ministry. I want to take this opportunity to highlight their importance in my life and open your eyes to additional ways in which He either has been or desires to communicate with you.

God drew my attention to numbers in 2001, but I didn't realize He was using them to speak to me until 2003. The ability to discern God's voice through numbers took off when I finally got that revelation. My attention was drawn to numbers on houses, cars, clocks, and televisions.

They captivated me as I learned their biblical meaning and significance, and I felt a pull from Holy Spirit letting me know He was speaking to me.

44 – My Chosen One

I was on my way back home to Los Angeles from Charlotte, North Carolina when God began showing me the number 44 to tell me I was His chosen vessel. My spirit was downcast at the time. God still had me in isolation, and His calling on my life was not evident to individuals I served alongside in ministry. Holy Spirit drew my attention to cabs as we made our way to the airport. These cabs had telephone numbers consisting of all 4's. The minute one passed, God immediately sent another to reinforce His message. My aunt began prophesying over my life as the cabs continued to pass us by. The moment was so powerful that my cousin circled the airport twice. A man with a white tub marked with the number 44 stood at the curb as we pulled up. Beloved, God had my attention. He drove home the point that it didn't matter if others couldn't sense His call upon my life through this experience. He used 44 to convince me that He not only called me, but He also chose me!

God expanded the number from 44 to 444 once I locked onto the revelation that I was His chosen vessel. The number 444 represents the end-time prophet, and that you are moving in the right direction. I sensed Holy Spirit telling me He was about to launch me into a new beginning. He told me it was time to call my former pastor to let him know He was leading me to launch More of God Global Ministries. He used 444 to push and affirm me. There were many times Holy Spirit drew my attention to clocks that read 4:44, and while doing hair, the temperature on my curling irons read 444. My mouth dropped when the pastor told me my meeting time. It was June 4 at 4:00 p.m. Beloved, God's message was clear!

$7,593--No Loan, Only God

I applied for a loan three times during the 2020 Coronavirus Pandemic and was denied each time. Though disappointed, I sensed God telling me He wanted to be the One to bless me. Yes, He could've blessed me with the loans, but He taught me something in the denial. I learned to whole-heartedly listen to Him and remain on His frequency, come what may. There was a moment when things got tight financially. I cried out to God in ways I hadn't in a long time. He gave me a vision of an open heaven one morning and told me He was about to send the rain.

Beloved, the very next day people began showering me with financial blessings. When it was all said and done, a total of 19 people sowed, which represents faith and manifestation, spiritual awakening, and growth. I was blessed with a total of $7,593. God is so amazing. Let me tell you the significance of this grand total. It's going to blow your mind.

The number 7 represents completion and perfection, 5 represents grace, 9 represents divine completion, and 3 represents the trinity. Each one of these numbers confirmed what God spoke to my spirit, and He used a financial blessing to drive the point home.

Beloved, there's never a dull moment with God. Just when you think you have Him all figured out, He reveals another facet of Himself. That's what He did for me with numbers. I pray that if you have never experienced the Lord communicating through numbers, the Holy Spirit would open your eyes and awaken you to this powerful form of communication from the Father to His children. It will bless you!

The following chart contains numbers the Lord frequently used to speak to me throughout my journey to Purpose. I pray you are blessed by what they reveal.

Biblical Meaning of Numbers

Number	Meaning
1	Unity, Godhead, New Beginning
2	Union, Division, Witness
3	Divine Completeness and Perfection, Trinity
4	Creation, The world, Creative Work
5	Grace, Fivefold Ministry
6	Man, Manifestation of Sin, Evils of Satan
7	Resurrection, Spiritual Completeness, Father's Physical and Spiritual Protection
8	New Birth and New Beginnings, New Order or Creation
9	Fruit of the Spirit and Divine Completeness from the Father
10	Testimony Law, Responsibility, Completeness of Order
11	Disorder, Judgement, Chaos
12	Perfect Government Foundation, God's Power & Authority, Perfection
13	Attributes of the Lord, New Beginnings, All the Government Created by Man & Inspired by Satan
14	Double meaning of 7 (Completion and Perfection), Deliverance and Salvation
15	Rest
16	Love
17	Victory Over the Enemy
18	Strength, Life
19	Faith, Manifestation, God's Perfect Order Regarding Biblical Judgement
20	Redemption
21	Sin, Weakness, New Beginnings
22	Human Relationships, Partnerships
33	Promise, Ministry
44	Chosen
55	Change
1111	Letting you know you're on the right path. The 11th hour, the last shall be first, Spiritual awakening
444	Letting you know you're on the right path; end times
555	Huge changes are up ahead. Trust that this transition is for your highest good, Things are getting exciting

ACKNOWLEDGEMENTS

I would like to give a huge "Thank You" to the following people:
My Husband, Brian Wilson; my Daughters (Dominique Wilson, Geonnie Wilson, LaToya Wilson), Rolando Juniel, Lynette R. Juniel, my Mother, Rosalea Robinson; my Father, Robert Robinson; Robert Juniel, Aunt Joan, Nevious Osborne, Aunt Janet Osborne, Dr. Susan Bradshaw, Roger Wilson, Iris Ude, Dorothy Williams, Karen Wallace, Jessica Mc Coy, Chelsea Douglas, Kashawn Obey, Ieashia Friend, Renee Hudson, Sonja Juniel, Meshell Juniel, Jasmann Smiths, Aunt Menette Young, Uncle Brad, Uncle Trent and family, Sydnie Jones, Kristy Hardiman, Dana Frelix, Dionne Hardiman – Huffman, Raven Rush, Kristal Green, Dr. LaQuesha Robinson, Nancy Prieto, Dr. Tracy Allen, Terry Didum, Serena Ellis, Juan Baraias, Peggy Jacobs, Lundon Love, Andrew Weitz, Eddie Batres, Andre Adrian Henry, Paulette Hawkins, The Doubletree Hospitality Event Staff in El Segundo, Bishop Peter Morgan, Pastor First Lady Morgan, and all of the many family members and friends who prayed for me to walk in my purpose.

NOTES

Introduction

i. "How to Wax a Car." *The Drive.Com*, 23 Sept. 2023, www.thedrive.com/cleaning-detailing/27319/how-to-wax-a-car. Accessed 5 May 2024.

Chapter 6

ii. "The 5 C's of Diamonds (Yes, 5): The Diamond Details You Don't Want to Miss."*Naturaldiamonds.Com*, 15 May 2025, www.naturaldiamonds.com/engagement-rings/5-cs-diamonds-guide/. Accessed 29 Jul. 2025.

iii. "The 4 C's of Diamonds: Evaluating Diamond Quality." *Diamonds.Pro*, 9 Jun. 2025 (Updated), www.diamonds.pro/education/4cs-diamonds/. Accessed 5 May 2024.

iv. [YouTube (Posted Originally by CNNMoney)]. (2024, May 5). See How Diamonds are Cut from Rocks [Video]. YouTube (Posted Originally by CNNMoney).https://www.youtube.com/watch?v=5O-LI_Pthu0o

v. "The 4 C's of Diamonds: What's Important When Buying Diamonds?" *Naturallycolored.Com*, www.naturallycolored.com/

diamond-education/diamond-grading/4cs-of-diamonds. Accessed 5 May 2024.

vi. "Is There Any Significance to Colors in the Bible?" *Christianity.com.* Accessed September 13, 2024, from https://www.christianity.com/ wiki/bible/is-there-any-significance-to-colors-in-the-bible.html

vii. (n.d.) Flawless Diamonds: Education and FAQ (includes explanation of diamond clarity and grading). Bluenile.com. https://www. bluenile.com/education/diamonds/clarity

viii. "The 5 C's of Diamonds (Yes, 5): The Diamond Details You Don't Want to Miss." *Naturaldiamonds.Com*, 15 May 2025, www.natural-diamonds.com/engagement-rings/5-cs-diamonds-guide/. Accessed 29 Jul. 2025.

ix. "The 5 C's of Diamonds (Yes, 5): The Diamond Details You Don't Want to Miss." *Naturaldiamonds.Com*, 15 May 2025, www.natural-diamonds.com/engagement-rings/5-cs-diamonds-guide/. Accessed 29 Jul. 2025.

ESV = English Standard Version
NLV = New Life Version

www.ingramcontent.com/pod-product-compliance
Lightning Source LLC
Chambersburg PA
CBHW031246120626
46545CB00007B/2677